My Mom, the Lawyer

by michelle browning coughlin, jd, msw

Copyright © 2019 Michelle Browning Coughlin, JD, MSW

All rights reserved.

No part of this publication may be reproduced, stored in a retrieval system, or transmitted in any form or by any means, electronic, mechanical, photocopying, recording, or otherwise, without the written permission of the author or her assigns.

MothersEsquire is the registered trademark of Mothers Esquire, Inc. The MothersEsquire logo is the trademark of Mothers Esquire, Inc.
www.motheresesquire.com

ISBN: 978-1-941953-94-5

Authored by Michelle Browning Coughlin, JD, MSW
Designed by Michelle Browning Coughlin using graphics from Canva.com; all copyright rights in images belong to the stock image artists

Printed in the United States of America

Published and distributed by Butler Books, www.butlerbooks.com

For Lane and Sloane,

with all my love,

Mom ❤

The printing of this book was sponsored by Kellie M. Barr, JD, a member of MothersEsquire, in loving memory of her grandmother, Ida Johnson. Ida's generosity led Kellie to create a "Do Good Fund" that Kellie uses to support organizations or people who are making a positive impact in the world.

My mom is a lawyer. Is your mom a lawyer, too? Have you ever thought about being a lawyer when you grow up?

Lawyers do so many different kinds of jobs. Come meet some of my friends and listen as they tell you all about their moms.

My mom is not a lawyer yet, but she will be soon.

During the week, we get ready to go to school together. When the school bus arrives, my mom squeezes me very tight and waves goodbye to me. Then she goes to law school.

Sometimes I go to law school with my mom . . .

and I sit very quietly while she listens. My mom does homework just like me. I like when we go to the library to do our work together.

My mom told me her teacher (she's called a professor) is a lawyer and a mom, too. She has a kid who is the same age as me!

I wonder if my mom will decide to be a law professor someday?

My mom is a lawyer. She's really smart and she worked hard to become a lawyer.

I like when I go to her office with her. My mom keeps crayons and markers in her desk, and she lets me hang my drawings on her wall.

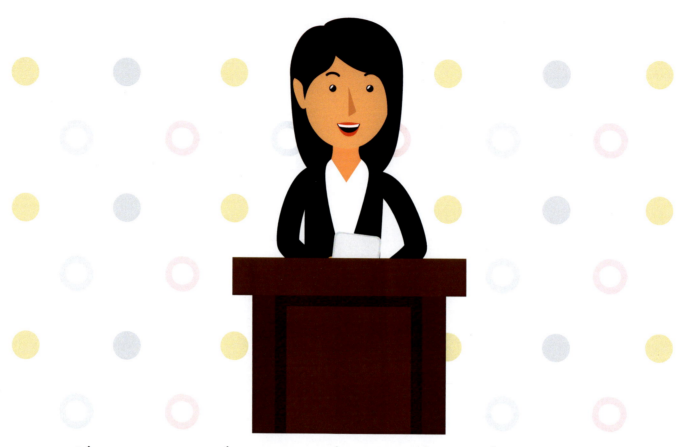

My mom is a lawyer and some days she goes to court. She helps people solve problems. She wears a suit and speaks in front of a judge and a jury.

My mom has to write papers for work called briefs and motions. She is a good writer. She helps me with my spelling words, and we like to make up stories together.

Some days my mom has to stay late at her office. And sometimes she stays up after I go to sleep to do more work.

But on other days . . .

my mom and I hang out at home in our pjs, and we build a fort in the living room with blankets. Then we drink hot chocolate together.

My mom is also a lawyer, but she does not go to a courthouse like the lawyers in movies. She works for a big company. She helps the company make good decisions.

My mom reads papers called contracts, and she writes lots of notes on them. Sometimes, she even helps my school read its contracts.

When my mom is at home, we take turns reading to each other. When she reads to me, she always uses really funny voices.

I wonder if she uses silly voices when she's reading contracts at work. That would be funny!

My mom is a lawyer in a really tall building downtown. She is called a partner.

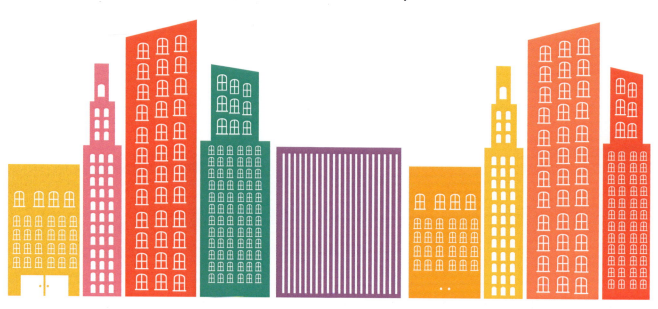

Right now, my mom is staying home with me and my new baby sister. Mom says she will stay home with us for a few months while my baby sister is very small.

After that, she said Daddy is going to stay home with us for a few months, and Mom will go back to work at her big building.

My dad stays home with me, too, while my mom is at work. We do errands sometimes, but some days we go to the zoo or the park. We have fun together!

My mom is a special kind of lawyer called a judge.

She sits in a courthouse and listens to cases. She hears about what happened to people and decides what to do.

One time, my mom could not come to my school program because she had to work on a really big case.

My grandpa got to come to my program instead. When I got home, Mom wanted to hear all about my day.

My mom is also a judge. When she is at work, she wears a long black robe. But when she is at home, she wears regular clothes, and we like to bake cookies together.

My mom is a military lawyer, and we live in a different country from where I was born. We moved here for my mom's job.

At first, I was scared about moving to a new place. But I really like it here. We are seeing new places, making new friends, and eating lots of new foods.

My mom is a lawyer, but she does not go to an office in a big building. She works at her desk at our house while I am at school.

Sometimes Mom goes on work trips. She packs her suitcase and flies on an airplane. When she gets home, she brings me pretzels from the plane. They are my favorite.

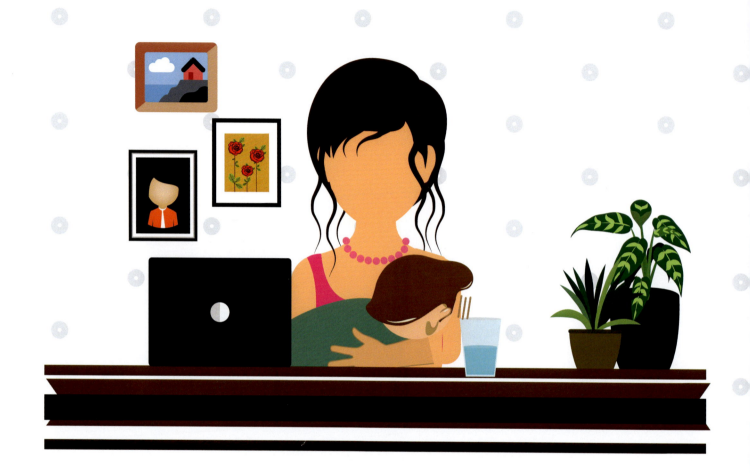

My mom owns her own law firm. She gets lots of emails and has meetings on her phone.

I like how my mom's voice sounds very important in her meetings. But when she sings songs to me at night, her voice sounds very soft.

My mom is a lawyer and she decided to run for a political office! She had a campaign and gave a lot of speeches.

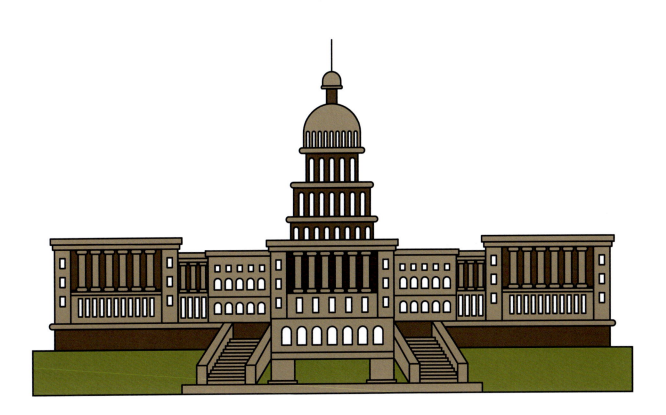

Since she is a lawyer, my mom knows a lot about laws. I think because she's a mom, she's very caring.

Being a mom and a lawyer makes her
a great leader!

When my mom ran for elected office, my brother and I helped her put up signs with her name on them.

She won, and now my mom goes to meetings and helps make the laws.

My mom is a lawyer, and she helps families. She tells me happy stories about helping little kids who needed a family.

Because she is a lawyer, my mom can go to court with families to help them with their adoptions.

I am really proud of my mom when she tells me stories about how she can help other people by being a lawyer.

Moms who are lawyers do so many different kinds of jobs! My mom shows me I can be anything. She teaches me about being a problem solver.

Having a mom who is a lawyer is pretty awesome.
And she says being my mom is definitely her
favorite job of all.

I've dedicated this book to my two wonderful daughters (who tagged along to law school with me!) and to all the lawyers of MothersEsquire. For all the lawyer-moms who work tirelessly as advocates for the rights of others, this book is for you. Simultaneously, these fierce leaders are raising the next generation of humans, either alone or with help from a partner or a village of family and friends. This book is dedicated to the mom-lawyers who found the legal profession filled with bias against mothers and ultimately took a different path, for now or forever. I dedicate this book to our military lawyers and their spouses, both men and women, who often must move from state to state or country to country. And, for the men who use their voices to ask for paternity leave, demand pay equality for their colleagues, and seek to be co-equal parents, thank you. And, of course, this book is for our most Honorable RBG, who lit the path and led the way.

Michelle Browning Coughlin, JD, MSW

About the author: Michelle Browning Coughlin is a mother of two daughters and a partner in a law firm in Louisville, Kentucky, practicing intellectual property and data privacy law. Michelle is the founder of MothersEsquire, a nonprofit organization devoted to gender equity in the legal profession, with a particular emphasis on support and advocacy for mothers and other caregiving lawyers. For more information about MothersEsquire, visit www.mothersesquire.com.